A PARENT'S GUIDE TO WATER POLO

First Edition

JOE GREENWALD

Copyright © 2014
by Joe Greenwald.
All rights reserved.

Published by Lulu Press, Inc.

Distributed by Lulu Press, Inc.

ISBN 978-1-312-05539-1

For all those who have sat in the stands with me, wondering what just happened and why every questionable call goes against our team, which inspired me to go home and read the rule book.

Contents

Introduction	1
Origins of Water Polo	7
Youth Water Polo	11
Understanding the Game	21
Water Polo Terminology	55
Water Polo After High School	69
Table 1 – Intercollegiate Programs	71
Table 2 - CWPA Men's Clubs	79
Table 3 – CWPA Women's Clubs	81
Table 4 – Community College Water Polo	83

Introduction

Water polo is a growing sport which challenges participants to achieve new levels of physical conditioning, work with others to succeed as a cohesive unit in a team sport, and be alert mentally to take advantage of changing game conditions. The sport, which has been played internationally for over a century, is experiencing increased popularity in the United States. The discipline required from athletes to train for and play water polo provides valuable life lessons. As a group water polo players tend to do well in the classroom. With the evolution of women's water polo over the last several decades both male and female athletes are now enjoying the competitive spirit and fun of the sport.
  A water polo game is contested by two teams, each with seven players in the water. Teams consist of six field players and one goalkeeper. Games take place in a pool, 20 to 30 meters in length, having a ten-foot wide by three-foot high goal at each end. The basic object is simple enough: score by getting a ball into the opponent's goal while preventing the opponent from scoring into your goal.

Playing a sport that is contested in the water with games that range in length from 20 to 34 minutes of playing time, water polo players must develop great physical conditioning. Water polo involves swimming up and down the pool, never touching the bottom, and battling with opponents to establish advantageous position while throwing, catching, and shooting a ball. It combines the aerobic conditioning of running, the physical play of wrestling, the team dynamics of basketball, and the emotion of football or soccer then puts it all in a swimming pool.

There is evidence that students participating in water polo also excel in the classroom. The NCAA uses a calculation called the Academic Progress Rate (APR) to measure the progress of student athletes at the university level. In a report that tracked Division I schools during the four year period ended 2012, water polo had the second highest average APR of all NCAA men's sports (exceeded only by Ice Hockey). On the women's side the sport achieved the same 980 score (on a 1,000 point scale) that the men's teams achieved.

A study looking at academic performance of athletes at UC Berkeley evaluated participants in ten sports. When ranked by Grade Point Average (GPA), women's water polo ranked second and men's water polo ranked fourth, both with average GPAs over 3.0.

While there is a lack of specific research on the correlation between water polo participation and academic performance in K-12, there is plenty to suggest there is a positive link. A 2013 University of Illinois at Urbana study found a positive correlation between aerobic fitness and academic retention and recall. A study conducted by researchers at Michigan State University determined that students who participated in vigorous sports did 10 percent better than their non-athletic peers in Science, English, Math, and Social Studies. The self-discipline and time management lessons learned from aquatics create skill sets that readily transfer to academic work. As you spend more time around water polo parents and coaches you are likely to hear many stories about the academic achievement levels of students participating in high school water polo.

Who Plays Water Polo?

Over the years many water polo players have gone on to make significant contributions to the world in a variety of different areas. There are actors, medical doctors, astronauts, athletes in other sports, firefighters, Navy SEALS, and a wide assortment of others that credit water polo with some of their early development. Some of the more famous names include:

- Actor **Ryan Bittle** who appeared in *Sweet Valley High*, *7th Heaven*, *Dawson's Creek*, *Shameless*, *The Closer*, and two separate stints on the long-running soap *All My Children*.
- Yogi and French Resistance participant **Gérard Blitz** who founded Club Med in 1950.
- Marine mammal trainer **Erin Bakey Brown** who works at Sea World in San Diego, California where she spends her days teaching marine mammals new behaviors and educating guests.
- News anchor **Josh Elliott** appears on the top rated morning show, *Good Morning America*, after a successful career at ESPN.
- Nobel Prize winner **Sir Alexander Fleming** who is known for his discovery of the first antibiotic, Penicillin.

- Nobel Peace Prize nominee **João Havelange** earned a law degree, serves as managing director of several companies, served on the International Olympic Committee, and was chairman of FIFA.
- Author and journalist **Ernest Hemingway** was one of America's most influential authors with notable works such as *For Whom the Bell Tolls* and *A Farewell to Arms*.
- Astronomer **Edwin Hubble** made a number of discoveries which proved the universe was far greater than previously believed and helped build the giant telescope on Palomar Mountain.
- Hawaiian Royal Family member **Duke Paoa Kahanamoku** became a pioneer in the sport of surfing, invented wind surfing, appeared in 29 movies, and served as Sheriff of Honolulu for 30 years.
- MIT mechanical engineering graduate **Jeff Ma** who was a member of the MIT Blackjack Team and was the basis for the main character of the book *Bringing Down the House* and the film *21*.
- Actor **Ted McGinley** who had roles on *Happy Days*, *The Love Boat*, *Married with Children* and *Hope & Faith*.
- Actress and model **Annalaina Marks** who appeared on *America's Next Top Model*, *Gossip Girl*, *Blue Bloods* and the feature film *Maid of Honor*.
- Greek shipping tycoon **Aristotle Onasis** was one of the richest men in the world and gained

Introduction

much public attention for his marriage to Jacqueline Kennedy, widow of US President John F. Kennedy.
- Grammy winning dancehall and reggae artist **Sean Paul** has been recognized with a variety of music awards and platinum records.
- Le Cordon Bleu trained chef **Rohan Rambukpotha** has served as Personal Chef to actors Adam Rodriguez and Mekhi Phifer and has cooked for the likes of the late Rosa Parks, former President Bill Clinton, Snoop Dogg, and Method Man.
- Astronaut **Steve Smith** has taken part in four different space missions covering over 16 million miles on the space shuttles Endeavour, Discovery, and Atlantis and conducted seven space walks totaling nearly 50 hours.
- Actor **Clayton Snyder** who played Ethan Craft on the hit Disney series *Lizzie McGuire* and the feature film *The Lizzie McGuire Movie*.
- 1984 *Time Magazine* Man of the Year **Peter Ueberroth** who organized the 1984 Los Angeles Olympics and served as commissioner of Major League Baseball.
- Olympic swimmer and actor **Johnny Weissmuller** who became famous for his part as Tarzan in the movie *Tarzan, the Apeman*.
- British royal family member **Prince William**, son of Prince Charles and the late Princess Diana, is second in the line of succession to the throne of the British Monarchy.

<u>Origins of Water Polo</u>

    The earliest origins of water polo are unclear. Some sources highlight water games that existed in many parts of the world in the late 19th century. These evolved into water festivals which were good for attracting crowds. Festivals taking place in Great Britain might include "water derby" in which contestants sat astride barrels to which a wooden horse's head was attached. By using make shift oars contestants could move their "horses" through the water. By adding a floating ball an element of the game of polo was introduced.
    More commonly, however, sports historians cite rugby football as the foundation for water polo. In this version early water polo contests took place in lakes and rivers. The object of this brutally physical game was merely to carry the ball to the opponent's side. In some versions a goal was scored when the ball was carried with two hands into a boat. However, one or two goal keepers could jump from the boat to prevent an opponent from scoring.
    Regardless of which version of history you believe, it is generally agreed that most of the early

origins of water polo took place in Great Britain. The word "polo" comes from the Balti word for ball, 'pulu', which the English pronounced 'polo'. In 1870, the London Swimming Association set down rules for "football to be played in a swimming pool." This game still looked more like rugby with a goal being scored by placing the ball, with two hands, on the deck. There was very little passing and a player attempting to score a goal still had to deal with a goalie jumping on him from the deck. A favorite trick of early water polo players was to hide the ball, which was five to nine inches in diameter, inside their swim suit, dive well below the surface in what could be very murky waters and then reappear as near to the goal as possible.

By 1880 new techniques coming out of Scotland began to put emphasis on passing, swimming, and scoring goals by throwing the ball into a cage that measured ten feet wide by three feet high. The free-for-all fighting that took place in early versions of the game was replaced by rules that limited "tackling" to the player with the ball and allowed players handling the ball to use just one hand at a time. These new rules would spread throughout Britain and form the foundation for a new set of standard rules.

In 1888, the London Water Polo League was founded and created formal rules that became the basis for the modern game. The first English championships took place in 1888 and the first international game was played in 1890 with England defeating Scotland, 4-0.

Between 1880 and 1890, water polo spread to other parts of Europe using the British rules. Teams began competing in Germany, Austria, France, Belgium, Hungary, and Italy.

Meanwhile, water polo took a different course in the United States. The first team is reported to have formed in 1888 at the Boston Athletic

Association. By 1890 teams were formed at Sydenham Swimmers Club in Providence, RI and at the New York Athletic Club (NYAC). The early American version of the game looked more like the old English style with an extremely physical approach to the game. This version used a soft, semi-inflated ball that could be carried underwater which further encouraged a game that looked more like rugby in the water.

Team sports were introduced to the Olympics at the 1900 games in Paris. Water Polo was included and took place on the River Seine. Nations were not represented at the time but seven clubs from four nations competed with the Osborne Swimming Club from Great Britain taking the gold medal in a single elimination tournament. Those Olympic games did not include a third place match so bronze medals were given to two clubs including Libellule de Paris which had a bye in the first round and lost its only game, 5-1, against eventual silver medalist Brussels Swimming and Water Polo Club.

The 1904 Olympics were held in St. Louis where water polo was contested using the more physical rules still being used in the United States at that time. Only three clubs entered, all from the United States. That tournament was not recognized as an Olympic event due to the lack of an international challenger. By the 1908 London Olympics teams represented their countries rather than clubs and water polo was contested in a pool. Great Britain would win the gold medal at the 1908, 1912, and 1920 Olympics (the 1916 games were cancelled).

FINA was founded in 1908 by eight national federations as an international body overseeing aquatics. By 1914 most US teams agreed to conform to the international rules used in other parts of the world. As 1928 approached there were 38 national federations participating in FINA. The organization led the formation of an international water polo committee in 1929. Rules developed for international games were put into effect in 1930 and FINA has been the governing body since that time.

The game has continued to evolve and will, no doubt, continue to change. In 1928 Hungary perfected the "dry pass" where the ball is passed from one player to another without touching the water. This contributed to Hungary dominating water polo competitions for many years. Californian Jimmy Smith's 1936 invention of a ball made with an inflatable bladder and a rubber fabric cover was an important change in the game.

International competition for women was introduced in 1978. The 2000 Olympics in Sydney saw the first women's competition in Olympic Water Polo with Australia defeating the United States in the gold medal game.

Rule changes that allow play to continue without interruption after a foul, allowing a direct shot form outside seven meters after a foul (which was changed to five meters in 2005), and the introduction of the exclusion foul to replace the older point system for fouls have allowed the game of water polo to continue its evolution.

Youth Water Polo

Your athlete's experience in water polo will vary depending on where he or she plays the game. At the same time, there are many components of the water polo experience that remain consistent regardless of where one chooses to learn and play the sport. It is common for water polo players to join a club and, when they are high school age, also play for their high school water polo team. The style and philosophies of the club you choose and the high school your son or daughter attends will impact your child's water polo experience.

Clubs

USA Water Polo is the predominant sanctioning body for club water polo in the United States. Another organizing body, American Water Polo, provides an alternative for clubs looking for a different approach.

USA Water Polo is broken into 11 geographic "zones". While California is by far the largest area in terms of number of clubs, water polo is played nationwide. The table on the next page shows the eleven zones and approximate percentage of USA Water Polo's close to 500 sanctioned clubs in each zone.

Central California	12%	Pacific Southwest	7%
Coastal California	17%	Pacific	15%
Midwest	5%	Southeast	8%
Mountain	5%	Southern Pacific	14%
Northeast	4%	Southwest	4%
Pacific NW/Hawaii	9%		

Much like other sports, the intensity, focus, and expectations of athletes varies by club. The age group programs available can also vary. While many clubs are large enough to have separate programs for boys and girls, some have mixed teams. For clubs running programs for younger athletes (10 years old and under), it is very common to have coed programs. Clubs will vary in their approach to which groups practice together. However, competition is typically broken into these levels:

- 10 and Under Coed
- 12 and Under Boys
- 12 and Under Girls
- 14 and Under Boys
- 14 and Under Girls
- 16 and Under Boys
- 16 and Under Girls
- 18 and Under Boys
- 18 and Under Girls

While it is not a lifetime commitment, selecting the right club is an important decision. Friendships will be formed and many hours will be spent in the pool with club teammates while working with club coaches; you want it to be a positive experience for your child. In most sports parents will tell you that the intensity level of the sport can vary widely depending on the approach of the coaching staff; water polo is no different. Some clubs are more serious about competing in, and winning, big tournaments, focusing on the best players, practicing more hours, and teaching more sophisticated game strategy. Other clubs may put more emphasis on teaching fundamentals and individual development. Most, if not all, clubs have some blend of these two priorities but will vary on the balance they strike. It is important to consider where your child is at in his or her development, the time commitment you wish to make, and your priorities for sports participation when selecting a club.

Other practical considerations you should think about include where the club practices, program cost, and other expenses the club may require. Some clubs use multiple pools so you should understand where your son or daughter will practice to start and where he/she is likely to practice in the future (it may or may not be the same pool). You may also want to evaluate the tournaments in which the club typically participates; some clubs will go longer distances to participate in more prestigious tournaments while others stay closer to home. You might like traveling or you might prefer to never leave the neighborhood but you are likely to have a better experience if you know your preferences and find a club that fits well with your priorities. Program cost is often driven by the number of practice hours each week as pool rental is one of the biggest expenses most clubs must cover. Other expenses you may be asked to cover include apparel (aside from team suit, clubs will vary on uniform expectations outside the pool such as team shirts, shorts, sweat suits, parkas, backpacks, etc.), travel to tournaments, banquets, and team events.

High School Water Polo

High school water polo is in a period of significant growth. The most rapid growth and largest participation base is in California where water polo continues to experience significant increases in participation. According to California Interscholastic Federation (CIF) figures, water polo was the fastest growing sport in the state, adding nearly 900 players from 2012 to 2013. Boys' water polo in the state grew by 4.3% while girls' water polo grew an impressive 2.8%.

Nationally, water polo is also growing. From 2008 to 2013 the number of high schools competing in boys' water polo grew from 698 to 789 with the number of participants growing from 18,032 to 21,943. Similarly, on the girls' side the number of schools competing has grown from 712 to 775 with participation growing from 17,773 to

18,674. Nationally, the overall growth rate for high school water polo has been 2.6% per year for the last five years, growing from 35,805 participants in 2008 to 40,617 participants in 2013.

Training

While the hours and intensity of training may vary by club or school, coach, age group, and season, there are basic areas of training that you can expect your child to experience. Swim workouts, strength training, skills work, and competition are important to the development of a water polo player.

Imagine a young child trying to play soccer, basketball, or baseball before knowing how to walk and run. It wouldn't make a whole lot of sense and the results would be disappointing. Swimming is as critical to water polo as running is to other sports. Many young athletes start out in swimming before moving to water polo. Whether a water polo player started out in swimming or not, he or she should expect to do a considerable amount of swim conditioning as part of his or her water polo training. It is common for practices to start or end with swimming laps; some coaches will put swimming at both the start and end of practice. During the water polo off-season, water polo clubs and high school teams often expect their players to participate in swim training. It is also not uncommon for water polo players to remain in, or join, swim clubs to enhance their swimming ability.

As with many other sports, strength training is important for the water polo player. However, the type and frequency of strength training can be expected to be very different for younger players than it is for older players. At the earliest ages strength training will likely consist of simple activities on the deck. Traditional push-ups and sit-ups might be all a very young player is occasionally asked to do at practice. Water polo players in high school will likely be required to attend regular workouts in the weight room with a higher level of intensity expected.

Skills work may encompass a wide range of drills generally taking place in the pool. Drills will focus on a variety of skills used by athletes when playing water polo: passing, catching, shooting, and establishing position. Similar to other team sports, time is likely to also be spent working on plays and special situations such as being up or down a player, counter attacks, or penalty throw cutoffs.

Competition is part of developing athletes in most sports and water polo is no exception. Some amount of scrimmaging is likely to take place in practice. But participation in tournaments and games against other teams and clubs is where the sport really comes to life. If your son or daughter is going to take part in water polo it is important to make the time to participate when there is an opportunity to play in a game or tournament.

Health and Injury

Water polo is considered a form of aerobic exercise. The conditioning associated with the sport uses all the major muscle groups and helps develop heart and lung strength. It combines bursts of speed and heavy effort with periods of lower intensity when players are treading water. According to Nutristrategy, a 130 pound water polo player will burn 590 calories per hour, while a 155 pound player will burn 704 calories per hour and a 180 pound player will burn 817 calories per hour.

It is important for a water polo athlete to have a well-balanced, healthy diet. Carbohydrate rich foods such as whole grain breads, cereals, pastas, rice, fruits, vegetables, and low-fat milk should be the primary source of calories as they provide fuel for the body. A carbohydrate rich snack prior to practice can help fuel muscles while carbohydrates after practice and games can help build energy stores for the next practice. Proteins, such as those found in fish, chicken, turkey, beef, pork, eggs, beans, milk, cheese, and yogurt are important for muscle recovery after games and practices; they are also important for growth and development of younger bodies. While water polo players are burning more calories than more sedentary peers, it is important that their increased calorie intake come from healthy foods. Consuming too much added sugar, processed foods, and snacks high in fat do not allow an athlete to maximize performance and creates eating habits that are a problem when the player is not training.

In addition to proper food intake, fluids are very important. It is natural to look at water polo and assume that dehydration is not an issue as the game is played in a large body of water! Players should be drinking fluids one to two hours before practice and make an effort to rehydrate every 20 minutes or so during activity. Water is generally a great selection though a sports drink with added carbohydrates and electrolytes may be a good choice during practice.

In addition to a good diet, rest is also important when putting in the training effort that an activity like water polo requires. It is important that the body gets appropriate sleep each night and also has periodic days off to allow full physical and mental recovery. Inadequate rest can lead to decreased performance and increased risk of injury.

Water polo is a physical sport and, like all sports, there is a risk of injury associated with participation in the sport. However, the frequency and severity of injuries in water polo appear to be less than those seen in other contact sports.

While there is a fair amount written about the types of injuries associated with water polo, there is limited statistical information available. But the data that is available leads to some insights. As stated in a 2011 San Diego Union Tribune article about water polo, "the risk of acute traumatic injury is less than football, and the frequency of chronic overuse injury is less than cross-country." A study by the Sports Academy Belgrade, where water polo has greater participation, compared the rate of injury of four men's sports. It found water polo to have the lowest frequency of injury behind basketball, volleyball, and soccer.

Generally, injuries resulting from participation in water polo are solved with rest and home care.

Occasionally an injury requires a visit to a medical professional. There are a number of specific injuries that are associated with water polo.

Shoulder Injuries

Throwing the ball is an integral part of playing water polo. When compared to other sports, the throwing motion in water polo is complicated by the lack of stable support from the legs which results from being in water rather than on a solid surface. This can lead to overuse injuries in and around the shoulder.

Most often shoulder injuries from water polo can be treated with rehabilitation exercises, ice, and rest. A focus on proper strength training of the core and shoulder muscles can help prevent shoulder injuries.

Knee Injuries

With most youth water polo players also participating in competitive swim, knee injuries are another area of concern. According to FINA, the international governing body for aquatic sports, 25% of all aquatic athletes will have knee pain some time during their competitive career. It is often referred to as "Breast Stroker's Knee" due to the higher frequency of occurrence in swimmers specializing in the breaststroke. The eggbeater kick used in water polo is also considered a contributing factor to the incidence of knee pain.

Ice and rest are the most common treatments of knee pain resulting from water polo activities. Physiotherapy, stretching, and strengthening activities, and, occasionally, pain relievers may also be prescribed. Surgical intervention is rarely required. Injury prevention activities should focus on proper hip flexibility and strengthening of the quadriceps and hamstring muscles.

Neck and Back Pain

Neck and back pain may result from the combination of spine rotation required for breathing in freestyle swimming and the twisting motion associated with throwing the ball. Fortunately, severe spine trauma is extremely rare and the injury is usually treated with rest. Emphasis on core abdominal and back strengthening exercises helps prevent neck and back pain resulting from water polo.

Hand and Finger Injuries

As with other sports that involve throwing and catching a ball, there is risk of hand and finger injuries in water polo. Most kids participating in sports involving a ball have at some time experienced the "jammed finger". An injury that results in a dislocation, deformity, inability to straighten or bend the finger, or significant pain warrants a visit to the doctor. Buddy taping, where the injured finger is taped to an adjacent finger, is often the only treatment that is required. Ice and anti-inflammatory medications may also be recommended.

Head Injury

In all sports today there is an increased emphasis on awareness of concussion and traumatic head injury. While there is limited statistical data on the frequency of head injuries in water polo, the research that has been conducted suggests the risks are not as high as in sports such as football or diving. However, a sport that involves throwing a ball and physical contact does create the potential for head injury. In the event of a concussion, or suspected concussion, coaches and parents should take a conservative approach and not allow the player to return to play until cleared by a doctor.

Other Injuries

A number of other minor issues may result from participation in water polo. In warmer climates where pools are outdoors, sunburn can be an issue. Clearly, use of sunscreen is appropriate when playing water polo in daylight. Like other activities that involve contact with others, occasional scratches and bruises can also result from playing water polo.

The significant amount of time spent by water polo players in chlorinated pools may lead to eye irritation or, with some players, skin irritation. These are easily solved with eye drops and rinsing off after being in the pool. Swimmer's Ear, the result of water creating a moist environment that aids bacteria growth in the outer ear canal, is another potential hazard of water polo; while generally not a serious health issue, it can be quite painful and become more serious if not addressed. Ear drops are usually recommended as a treatment and may be used more regularly by athletes that have a history of issues with Swimmer's Ear.

Understanding the Game

Anyone who has attended a water polo tournament knows that one clue to finding the pool when you're at a new location is to listen for referees' whistles. Water polo contests are noteworthy for the seemingly constant blowing of whistles to keep the game on track.

For the uninitiated that means there's a lot going on and no announcer there to explain it. Over time you will pick-up much of the game from other parents who, for the most part, never played the game and have not read the rule book. You will most likely also learn from these parents that there are a lot of bad calls in water polo and every one of them goes against your team (it is an extremely rare moment when a parent says, "Wow, we got a break there!").

Water polo is a physical sport and there is a lot of contact between players. The type of contact that is allowed is controlled by the situation and the position of the players. When there is a foul it can either be "common" or "major". Typically, in both cases, play resumes immediately so there's not a lot of time for asking questions and learning (or even noticing what just happened).

Much like basketball, players in front of the goal are fighting for position. In this battle there are things that are legal and things you aren't allowed to do. Much like the passing rules in football, there is contact that is legal only when an opponent is in possession of the ball.

Similar to soccer and hockey, there is a line you cannot cross unless the ball has already crossed that line. Many of the concepts of water polo can be compared to other sports; what makes it most intriguing is that in water polo it all takes place in...water!

As is also true in other sports, there are variations in water polo rules at different levels of competition. Similar to football where NFL rules require two feet in bounds for a catch while college only requires one foot in bounds, or baseball which uses a designated hitter in the American League while pitchers bat in the National League, there are variations in the rules of water polo. Rule-making organizations you may hear about in water polo include:

- FINA (Federation Internationale de Natation) is the international governing body for water sports such as water polo, swimming, diving, synchronized swimming, and open water events. It is responsible for the rules of international water polo including competitions such as the Olympics and World Championships.
- USA Water Polo sets the rules for all USA Water Polo sanctioned events in the United States including Men's and Women's National Championships. Many youth clubs in the United States regularly participate in tournaments that are sanctioned by, and adhere to the rules of, USA Water Polo. USA Water Polo rules closely mirror the FINA rules.
- The NCAA (National Collegiate Athletic Association) is the predominant association for university athletics. As such, it sets the rules for most sports that it sanctions, including men's and women's water polo.
- NFHS (National Federation of State High School Associations) publishes rules that are frequently used in high school competition.

While each organization can have its own rule variations, the rules for water polo used across these organizations are consistent enough that one can gain a basic understanding of the sport without having to be an expert on the subtleties of the rules across governing bodies.

It should also be noted that late in 2013, FINA made some notable modifications to its rules. Only time will tell if other organizations adapt the same rules and how significantly the rule modifications will impact officiating and actual play.

The intent of this section is not to make you an expert at water polo rules. However, having a basic understanding of the game will make it more enjoyable and, perhaps, make you feel less like your athlete is being victimized by referees that are letting the other team get away with everything.

So, put on your white polo shirt, white pants, and white deck shoes, and you can act like a water polo referee while you review the basic rules.

The Pool and Markings

The distance between goal lines for international competition is between 20 and 30 meters (approximately 65 to 98 feet) for men; and between 20 and 25 meters (approximately 65 to 82 feet) for women. There is an additional .3 meters (1 foot) beyond the goal line that is part of the field of play. The width of the field of play is between 10 and 20 meters.

High school fields are ideally 25 meters by 20 meters but 25 yard pools are often used. In either case the width of the field should be between 13 and 20 meters (43-66 feet).

The goal itself should be 3 meters in width (approximately 10 feet). If the pool is at least 1.5 meters (5 feet) deep, the underside of the crossbar on the goal should be .9 meters (3 feet) from the water. Although far less common, if the pool is shallow (less than 1.5 meters deep), the underside of the cross bar should be 2.4 meters (approximately 8 feet) from the floor of the pool. High school rules suggest the minimum depth of the pool should be two meters (6 feet 6 inches).

You should also see a series of markings along the side of the pool. Ideally, the deck along the side of the water will be painted but you may also see wooden markers that are placed on the deck only during water polo events, pylons (cones) or other such markers. Whatever the marking style, the colors you should see include:

- White – at the goal line and the half distance line (middle of the field of play)
- Red – two meters from the goal lines
- Yellow – five meters from the goal line.

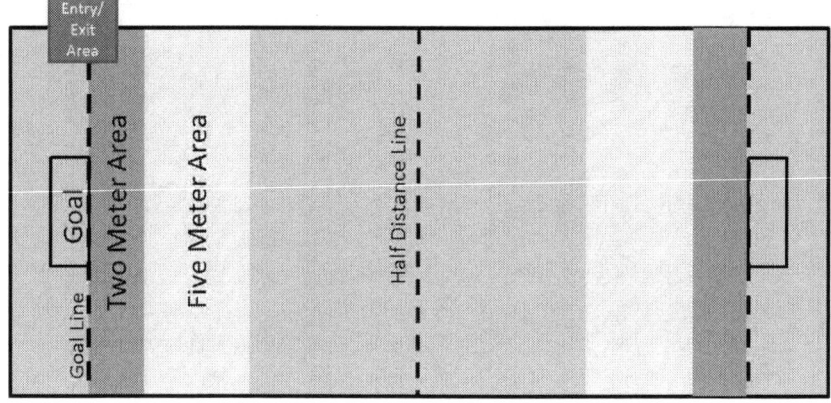

Caps

At all levels of water polo players are required to wear caps. In college and high school, the home team wears dark caps while the visiting team wears white caps. Goalies wear red caps or paneled caps that alternate red with the team color. USA Water Polo and FINA rules call for goalie caps to be either number 1 or number 13. All other numbers are field players. College rules require goalie caps to be numbered 1, 1A, 1B, etc.

Understanding the Game

Game Structure

Regardless of the sanctioning body, the game of water polo is broken into four quarters. Two minute breaks take place between the first and second quarters as well as between the third and fourth quarters. Between the second and third quarters there is a five minute break.

The length of quarters varies by level and tournament. For international and collegiate competitions the length of quarters is eight minutes. In high school quarters typically last seven minutes for varsity games, six minutes for junior varsity games, and five minutes for frosh/soph games. For other tournaments, such as youth club competition, the length of quarters will be set by the host organization and may vary by age group and round of the tournament.

Each team is allowed timeouts which, depending on the level and tournament rules, are usually one or two minutes in duration. Typically, high school and collegiate teams are allowed three timeouts during the course of the game but this may vary by tournament or level. If there are overtime periods it is usual for each team to be allowed one timeout (unused timeouts from regulation play do not carry over).

For international competition and tournaments falling under FINA or USA Water Polo guidelines, rule changes in late 2013 set timeouts at one per quarter with timeouts no longer being cumulative (unused timeouts do not carry over to subsequent quarters).

Players and Substitutes

There are seven players in the pool for each team. Six field players and the goalie who must wear the goalie cap.

Typically, substitutions take place when there is a break in the action. In the following cases the substitute may enter the field of play from any place:

- between quarters or between extra periods
- after a goal has been scored

- during a time out
- when replacing a player who is bleeding or injured.

Although less common, substitutions may be made at any time during the game including during live action. However, in these cases the players must enter and exit through the "re-entry" area nearest their own goal line. The re-entry area is generally the corner of the pool in front of the team's bench.

Start of Play

There are different methods for determining which end of the pool each team starts from. It may be done by a coin flip before the start of the game as NCAA rules outline. FINA rules call for the team assigned white caps to start to the left of the scorer's table.

At the start of each period players line-up on their respective goal lines about one meter apart and at least one meter from the goal posts. No part of a player's body may be beyond the goal line at water level. There may not be more than two players between the goal posts.

The referee's whistle signals the start of the sprint with the ball put into play on the half distance line. Most often the referee drops the ball into the pool from the side of the deck. However, you will occasionally see the ball put in the center of the pool with a device that holds it in place until play is started.

The game clock starts when a player touches the ball.

Scoring a Goal

The simple object of water polo is to score more goals than the other team. So, the rules defining the scoring of a goal are important!

A goal is scored when the entire ball has passed FULLY over the goal line, between the goal posts and underneath the cross bar. It is not uncommon for the ball to partially (even mostly) cross the goal line without being fully across.

Understanding the Game

Goals can be scored from anywhere within the field of play with the exception that the goal keeper is not permitted to go, or touch the ball, past the half distance line. A goal can be scored by any part of the body except a clenched fist. Thus, it is possible for a player to "dribble" the ball all the way into the goal.

Also, at the start of the game or any restart, at least two players must intentionally play or touch the ball (may be players from either team except the defending goal keeper). Exceptions to this part of the rule include: 1) a penalty throw; 2) a free throw thrown by a player into the player's own goal; 3) an immediate shot from a goal throw; 4) an immediate shot from a free throw awarded outside 5 meters.

A goal counts if it is in the air as the shot clock or game clock expires and enters the goal. As it pertains to this rule, if the ball enters the goal after hitting the goal post, crossbar, goalkeeper or other defending player, and/or bounces off the water, the goal is still allowed. If the ball lands in the water and then floats completely over the goal line, the goal counts only if the ball floats over the goal immediately due to the momentum of the shot.

If the referee blows a whistle for a foul while the ball is in flight to the goal, a goal is not scored even if the ball crosses the goal line. Similarly, if it is discovered there is a player in the pool with three fouls when a goal is scored, the goal is not counted. Also, if the goalkeeper drops the ball into his own goal on a goal throw or free throw, no goal is counted; the goalkeeper is allowed to take the throw again.

After a goal, the game is restarted with players taking up positions anywhere in their respective halves of the field of play. No part of a player's body is allowed beyond the half distance line. Actual play resumes after the referee blows his/her whistle and the ball leaves the hand of a player on the team that gave up the goal.

Shot Clock

Much like basketball, water polo employs the use of a shot clock. At most levels of the game the shot clock is

30 seconds. However, you will occasionally see longer shot clocks (typically 35 seconds); this is most likely to occur in the youngest age brackets of a youth water polo tournament.

The shot clock is reset when:

- the ball leaves the hand of a player taking a shot. If the ball does not go into the goal and rebounds into the playing area, the shot clock does not resume until the ball comes into possession of one of the teams. Practically speaking, many timers will reset the shot clock on the shot and let it run; they then reset the clock again when one of the teams gains possession.
- the opposing team gains possession of the ball. Merely touching a ball in flight, however, does not constitute possession. The opponent must actually gain control of the ball.
- the ball is put into play following an exclusion foul, penalty foul, goal throw, corner throw, or neutral throw. However, under FINA rules as modified in 2013, simultaneous exclusion fouls to players on opposing teams do not result in a reset of the shot clock (unless neither team had possession of the ball).

Goal Throws

Goal throws are awarded when the entire ball passes the goal line without going into the goal, having last been touched by any player other than the goalkeeper of the defending team. A goal throw is also awarded when the ball goes into the goal from: 1) a free throw awarded inside the five meter line; 2) a free throw awarded outside of five meters that is not taken immediately; 3) a corner throw.

Goal throws are given to the team on defense and are taken from inside the two meter area. While most often made by the goalie, the throw can legally be made by any player near the ball. Further, the "throw" does not necessarily need to be made to another player, though this is most often the case. The throw merely needs to be made in a way that other players can see the ball leaving the hand of the player making the throw. This is sometimes accomplished by tossing the ball into the air or dropping it to the water from a raised hand.

When a player is awarded a goal throw, the defense may not attempt to play the ball before it has left the hand of the thrower. The defender is also generally expected to stay an arm's length distance away from the player making the goal throw.

Corner Throws

A corner throw is awarded when the entire ball passes the goal line, without going into the goal, having last been touched by the goalkeeper of the defending team; most often this occurs when the goalkeeper blocks a shot and it goes out of the playing area. A corner throw is also awarded when a defending player deliberately sends the ball over the goal line.

The corner throw is taken by a member of the attacking team from the two meter mark on the side of the pool nearest to where the ball crossed the goal line. Similar to goal throws, the throw merely needs to be made in a way that other players can see the ball leaving the hand of the player making the throw. Just like the goal throw this is sometimes accomplished by tossing the ball into the air or dropping it to the water from a raised hand.

When a player is awarded a corner throw the defense may not attempt to play the ball before it has left the hand of the thrower. Obviously, this precludes the defender from making any contact with the player making the corner throw. While the defender may still raise an arm in front of a player taking a corner throw, his arm needs to be behind his/her head. The defender is also expected to stay an arm's length distance away from the player making the corner throw.

Neutral Throw

A neutral throw is used when it is not clear who should have possession of the ball. This can occur in a number of circumstances:

- when, at the start of the period, the referee feels that the ball fell into a position to give an advantage to one team over the other (that is, it didn't land on the half distance line)
- when one or more players from opposing teams commit an ordinary foul at the same time
- when both referees blow their whistles at the same time to award ordinary fouls to opposing teams
- when neither team has possession of the ball and one or more players from opposing teams commit an exclusion foul at the same time
- when the ball hits an overhead obstruction.

A neutral throw involves the referee throwing the ball into the field of play at approximately the same lateral position as where the event occurred. It's done in such a manner as to allow players of both teams to have equal opportunity to reach the ball. It is similar in concept to a face-off in hockey or a jump ball in basketball except that it's done in the water. A neutral throw awarded inside two meters is taken on the two meter line.

Free Throw

A free throw is awarded as the result of an ordinary foul (ordinary fouls are explained in the next section).

The free throw takes place at the spot where the foul occurred with the exception of certain situations:

- if the ball is further from the defending team's goal than where the foul occurred, the free throw is taken from the location of the ball

- if the foul is committed by a defending player inside his/her own two meter line, the free throw takes place from the two meter line (if the ball is outside the two meter line in this situation, the free throw is taken from the location of the ball).

Free throws must be taken within a reasonable time frame (at the discretion of referee). It is an offense if a player who is most readily in a position to take a free throw does not do so (this results in a free throw for the other team).

As with other throws described above, it is not necessary for the throw to go to another player. It just needs to be done in a way that other players can observe the ball leaving the hand of the player taking the throw. The ball is immediately in play as soon as it leaves the hand of the player taking the free throw.

When a player is awarded a free throw the defense may not attempt to play the ball before it has left the hand of the thrower. Obviously, this precludes the defender from making any contact with the player making the free throw. While the defender may still raise an arm in front of a player taking a free throw, his arm needs to be behind his/her head. The defender is also generally expected to stay an arm's length distance away from the player making the free throw (when a free throw is awarded at the set position the defender just needs to give enough room to demonstrate there is no undue interference with the ability of the set to make a free throw).

FINA's 2013 rules updates further specify that the defender must move away from the player taking the free throw prior to putting a hand up. While the new rule does not specify how far away the defending player must move, early interpretations suggest it should be at least one meter.

Fouls

For someone new to the game of water polo, one of the most noticeable aspects of the game is the frequency of whistles with no clear stoppage in play. In football a play is over when the whistle blows with the teams lining-up again before play resumes. Similarly, in basketball play stops when the whistle blows and there is a formality to play resuming with an inbound pass, players lining-up for a free throw, or a jump ball.

When the referee blows the whistle in water polo play frequently continues without any clear interruption. Again, unlike other sports, fouling is often a good strategy in water polo, further adding to the frequency of foul calls.

As a spectator it is important to have some understanding of the rules associated with fouls when watching water polo. This understanding will give you a better appreciation for what is taking place in the water and reduce feelings that your athlete is not receiving fair treatment from the game officials!

There are three general types of fouls in water polo:

- Ordinary Fouls
- Exclusion Fouls
- Penalty Fouls

Ordinary Fouls

Players are called for ordinary fouls when they violate a "minor" rule. Minor fouls result in a Free Throw (Free Throws are explained in previous section). The time between the calling of the foul and the "free throw" is generally no more than a few seconds. Play does not stop when an ordinary foul is called; players on both teams continue to swim and establish position for the play.

Some of the violations that result in a free throw include:

- A player advancing beyond the goal line at the start of a period prior to the referee giving the signal to start. The free throw is taken from the location of the ball or, if the ball has not yet been released into the field of play, from the half distance line.
- Holding on to, or pushing off from, goal posts or ends of pool during actual play or at the start of a

Understanding the Game

period. However, in a 25 yard pool where players line-up on the wall to start each quarter they may push off of the side of the pool.
- To take an active part in the game while standing on the bottom of the pool, to walk when play is in progress, or to jump from the floor of the pool to play the ball or tackle an opponent. This rule does not apply to the goalkeeper when he/she is within the five meter area.
- Taking or holding the entire ball under water when tackled; commonly referred to as "ball under." It is still a minor foul if the player holding the ball has the ball forced under water as the result of an opponent's challenge (it does not matter that the ball goes under water against the player's will). A ball under call should go against the team in possession of the ball even if it is actually pushed under water by a defender. If a player holds the ball under water but is not being tackled there is no foul. If the ball is held under water for only a fraction of a second it is not a ball under foul.
- Striking at the ball with a clenched fist. This rule does not apply to the goalkeeper when he/she is within the five meter area.
- Playing or touching the ball with two hands at the same time. This rule does not require contacting the ball with two hands, merely attempting to play it with two hands. Thus, players putting hands up to block a shot may only put up one hand. This rule does not apply to the goalkeeper when he/she is within the five meter area.
- Impeding or otherwise preventing the free movement of an opponent who is not "holding" the ball, including swimming on the opponent's shoulders, back, or legs. "Holding" the ball is lifting, carrying, or touching the ball but does not

include dribbling the ball. A player holding the ball can also be called for impeding if he is preventing the free movement of an opponent. For international games, and games using USA Water Polo guidelines, rule changes in 2013 now make this an exclusion foul (described in section below).
- Pushing or pushing off from an opponent who is not holding the ball.
- Being within two meters of the opponent's goal line. It is not uncommon to hear fans or coaches yelling "inside two meters" when they feel an opponent is violating this rule. However, players are allowed in this area if they possess the ball or if the ball is closer to the goal line than the player. Once the ball leaves the two meter area, usually the result of a pass, players inside the two meter area must also leave the area. However, if a player passes the ball from the two meter area to another player who immediately shoots the ball, there is not a penalty against the player in the two meter area.
- Taking too long to put the ball in play on a free throw, goal throw, or corner throw. If a player takes too long to put the ball in play, more than a few seconds at the referee's discretion, it becomes a free throw for the other team.
- Wasting time. In its 2013 rules update, FINA expanded the "wasting time" rule to state that if the goalkeeper is the only member of the team in that team's half of the field of play it shall be deemed wasting time for another member of the team to pass the ball back to the goalkeeper. The update also clarified that teams must progress the ball forward in the field of play; if, during the last 30 seconds of the game, the team with the ball makes no effort to progress the ball forward the referee should immediately award an ordinary foul.

Understanding the Game

- Being the last to touch the ball before it goes out the side of the field in play. If, however, a defensive player blocks a shot out of the field of play, the free throw goes to the defensive team.
- Taking action to "simulate a foul" in the hopes of getting a foul call against the opponent. If a team repeatedly simulates fouls the referee may issue a yellow card warning to the team and, ultimately, may make a "misconduct" call against a player.

Exclusion Fouls

More serious violations of the rules result in an exclusion foul. A player called for an exclusion foul is required to leave the field of play via the team's re-entry area. The player is not replaced and his/her team continues play with one less player in the field of play, frequently referred to as "being a man down" or a "6-on-5". The offended team also receives a free throw. The player exiting the pool must do so without interfering with play.

As with a free throw as described above, play does not stop when an exclusion foul is called; players on both teams continue to swim and establish position for the play. However, under FINA rules as modified in 2013, play does not resume after an exclusion foul inside the five meter area until the referee signals the restart of play with an upward movement of the hand.

The excluded player must remain in the re-entry area until: 1) the other team scores a goal; 2) 20 seconds of playing time elapses; or 3) his/her team gains possession of the ball. If simultaneous exclusions are called against opposing players, both players are excluded for 20 seconds.

If an excluded player intentionally interferes with play, or fails to commence leaving the field of play almost immediately, a penalty throw will be awarded to the opposing team. Further, the offending player receives another personal foul.

Some of the violations that may result in an exclusion foul include:

- A player leaving the water or sitting or standing on steps or side of pool during play. Exceptions to this rule include accident, injury, illness, or with permission of the referee.
- Interfering with a free throw, goal throw, or corner throw. This includes intentionally throwing away the ball, or failing to release it, to prevent the normal progress of the game. It also includes any attempt to play the ball before it has left the hand of the thrower. In its 2013 rule updates, FINA further clarified that a defending player must move away from the player taking the free throw before raising an arm to block a shot or pass (while a distance is not specified, FINA commentary suggests there should be one meter of separation).
- Attempting to block a pass or shot with two hands when outside the 5 meter area.
- Intentionally splashing the face of an opponent.
- Holding, sinking, or pulling back an opponent who is not holding the ball.
- Intentionally kicking or striking an opponent.
- Failure of the defending goalkeeper to take the correct position on the goal line for a penalty throw after being ordered by the referee to do so. Another defending player may replace the goalkeeper but without the goalkeeper's privileges, such as attempting to block the shot with both hands.
- An excluded player, or substitute player, entering the field of play improperly. This includes not receiving a signal from the referee, entering from a place other than the player's own re-entry area, jumping or pushing off from side or wall of pool, or affecting the alignment of the goal. If this penalty is called against the team on defense, the offending

Understanding the Game

player is excluded and the opposing team receives a penalty throw.
- Interfering with the taking of a penalty throw. In this case the offending player is excluded from the remainder of the game and the penalty throw is retaken by the opposing team.
- Committing an act of brutality against another player or official. Brutality includes playing in a violent manner, or kicking or striking with a malicious intent. When brutality is called during the game the offending player is excluded for the remainder of the game. The offending player may be substituted when four minutes of actual play have elapsed. If the foul took place during play a penalty throw is awarded. In the case where simultaneous brutality calls are made against opposing players, each team will shoot a penalty throw. If the incident occurs when play is stopped (such as between periods, during a timeout, etc) no penalty throws are awarded.
- In high school and college, players can be excluded for minor acts of misconduct. These are generally minor comments to the referee, such as "Call the foul", minor gestures to the referee or other players, or minor taunting. The first such foul results in a 20 second exclusion with immediate substitution. A subsequent minor act of misconduct results in exclusion for the remainder of the game. Note: the use of profanity or obscene language is considered misconduct and the first occurrence results in exclusion of the offending player for the remainder of the game.
- Under 2013 FINA rule changes for international games and games using USA Water Polo guidelines, impeding or otherwise preventing the free movement of an opponent who is not "holding" the

ball, including swimming on the opponent's shoulders, back, or legs. "Holding" the ball is lifting, carrying, or touching the ball but does not include dribbling the ball. A player holding the ball can also be called for impeding if he is preventing the free movement of an opponent.
- Under FINA rules as of 2013, using two hands to hold an opponent anywhere in the field of play.
- Also under FINA rules as of 2013, upon a change of possession a defending player committing a foul on any player of the attacking team anywhere in the attacking team's half of the field of play.

Penalty Fouls

Some fouls result in the opposing team being awarded a penalty throw.

A penalty throw can be taken by any player, with the exception of the goalkeeper, on the team to which the penalty was awarded. The penalty throw can be taken from anywhere on the five meter line (generally, it's taken from the middle of the five meter line).

All other players leave the five meter area and must be at least two meters away from the player taking the throw. On each side of the player taking the throw, the defending team has the first right to take that position. The defending goalkeeper must be positioned between the goal posts with no part of his body beyond the goal line at water level (in a pool with wall mounted goals, the goalie's hips may not be beyond the goal line). It is very common to see the referee backing the goalkeeper up to the appropriate spot prior to a penalty throw. If the goal keeper is out of the water, another player may take the position of the goalkeeper but does not have the same privileges as the goalkeeper (such as using two hands while attempting to block the ball).

When the referee signals for the throw to be taken (by blowing the whistle and dropping a raised arm), the player taking the throw must immediately throw it with an uninterrupted movement directly at the goal. While the

Understanding the Game

player may not use any type of pump fake, it is acceptable to take the ball backwards from the direction of the goal in preparation for the throw as long as the continuity of the movement is not interrupted before the ball leaves his/her hand. Failure to execute the throw properly results in a goal throw for the defending team.

Once a penalty throw is taken the ball is in play. If the ball rebounds from the goal post, crossbar, or goalkeeper it remains in play. In this case it is not necessary for another player to play or touch the ball before a goal can be scored.

If a penalty foul is called in the last minute of the game, second overtime period, or during "sudden-victory" overtime periods of a high school game, the coach may elect to retain possession of the ball rather than take the penalty throw. In this case, the team is awarded a free throw on or behind the half distance line with a new possession clock.

Situations in which a penalty throw is awarded include:

- Any foul committed by a defending player within the five meter area in a situation where "a goal probably would have resulted."
- A defender or the goalkeeper pulling down or displacing the goal. In the case where a player pulls the goal over completely with the intent of preventing a probable goal, the offending player is also excluded from the remainder of the game.
- A defending player, other than the goalkeeper, attempting to block a shot or pass with two hands while in the five meter area.
- Using a clenched fist to play the ball. The goalkeeper is excepted from this rule.
- The goalkeeper or other defending player taking the ball under water when tackled.
- A defending player within the five meter area kicking or striking an opponent or committing an

act of brutality. In the case of brutality, in addition to the penalty shot, the offending player is excluded for the remainder of the game with a substitute allowed only after four minutes of play have elapsed.

- An excluded player intentionally interfering with play.
- Under FINA rules, a coach or other official of the team not in possession of the ball requesting a timeout (this does not result in a personal foul as described below).
- Also under FINA rules, a coach or team official taking any action with intent to prevent a probable goal or to delay the game.

Personal Fouls

A personal foul is recorded against a player any time he/she commits an exclusion foul or a penalty foul. Once a player has three personal fouls, the player is excluded from the remainder of the game. A substitute, however, may be inserted into the game. Ordinary fouls do not count toward the three personal foul limit.

Goalkeeper Privileges/Limitation

The goalkeeper, identified as the player wearing the goalkeeper cap, is allowed to do some things other players are not allowed to do. These include:

- Striking the ball with a clenched fist. Typically, a goalkeeper may do this when blocking a shot.
- Standing on, and pushing off from, the bottom of the pool.
- Attempting to play or touch the ball with two hands at the same time.

These privileges apply only when the goalkeeper is inside the five meter area. If the goalkeeper attempts to use these privileges outside the five meter area it is an ordinary foul.

On the flip side, the goalkeeper has one limitation. He/she is not permitted to go past the half distance line. Doing so constitutes an ordinary foul.

A substitute goalkeeper, a player replacing the original goalkeeper and wearing a goalkeeper cap, has the same privileges and limitation as the original goalkeeper. However, a field player defending the goal, such as when the goalkeeper is serving an exclusion penalty, does not receive the same privileges.

Advantage Rule

A short, but very significant, rule in water polo deals with "Advantage." It states:

> "The referees shall refrain from declaring a foul if, in their opinion, such declaration would be an advantage to the offending player's team. The referees shall not declare an ordinary foul when there is still a possibility to play the ball.
>
> "[Note: *The referees shall apply this principle to the fullest extent. They should not, for example, declare an ordinary foul in favour of a player who is in possession of the ball and making progress towards his opponents' goal, because this is considered to give an advantage to the offender's team.]*"

While this rule is short, it merits many pages of discussion in the officiating manual. The manual discusses "advantage" and "relative advantage." For example, a six on five advantage situation is generally not as good as a two on one advantage. So, if a defender commits a foul in a two-on-one situation, the referee may not call the foul if he believes it will stop play long enough to take away that advantage and leave the attacking team with a six-on-five. However, if the defensive foul eliminates the two-on-one advantage then the referee should call the foul to restore the offensive advantage to six-on-five.

In its 2013 update to the rules, FINA modified this simple rule to add more clarity:

> "The referees shall have discretion to award (or not award) any ordinary, exclusion or penalty foul, depending on whether the decision would advantage the attacking team. They shall officiate in favour of the attacking team by awarding of a foul or refraining from awarding a foul if, in their opinion, awarding the foul would be an advantage to the offending player's team.
>
> "[Note. The referees shall apply this principle to the fullest extent.]"

Within the concept of advantage, three types of "advantage" are discussed in the officiating manual:

- Possessional Advantage
- Positional Advantage
- Probable Goal Advantage

Possessional Advantage

Possessional advantage exists when a player *"has the ball and can do something with it."* Players do NOT have possessional advantage when they receive bad passes, do not have full control of the ball, or are pinned to the side of the pool at midtank or down at the two meter line by good defense.

If a defensive player violates a rule to take away possessional advantage then an ordinary foul should be called. Awarding a free throw returns possessional advantage to the offensive team. However, if an offensive player loses possessional advantage due to poor play there should rarely be a foul called.

In addition to individual possessional advantage, the official's manual discusses the concept of team possessional advantage. If a player is being fouled but still has the ability to make a good pass to an open teammate a foul should NOT be called as the stoppage of play would take away the team advantage. In that same situation, however, if the player's ability to make the pass is taken away by the defender's actions then an ordinary foul should be called.

During a game, situations can change rapidly. A defender may be fouling a player at midtank but there is no call because the player with the ball can't do anything with it; that is, there is not possessional advantage. But if a teammate swims into position to receive a pass there is now possessional advantage because the pinned player now has someone to whom the ball can be passed. So, in this situation, a foul should be called because the offense now has a possessional advantage.

Positional Advantage

The next level of advantage is positional advantage. There are two basic types of positional advantage for the offense: 1) an attacking player is in position to advance the ball into scoring position regardless of whether or not that person actually has possession of the ball; or 2) when the defender is not in position to defend the goal. The defense can also have positional advantage to which referees must also pay attention.

An obvious example of positional advantage is when the head of an attacking player is closer to the goal than the defender's head. Take the situation of an offensive player leading a break being a half body ahead of the defender. The defender pulls back on the attacker at about six meters. If the attacker loses position relative to the defender, the defender took away positional advantage by holding and pulling back on a player not holding the ball. A foul should be called.

If in that same situation, however, the attacker is still able to make relatively unimpeded progress toward the goal, the holding has not altered the positional advantage of the attacking player. No foul should be called. In fact, calling a foul would be wrong as it would take advantage away from the attacker who would now have to execute a free throw, basically taking that attacker out of a potential scoring position. By holding off on the call, the referee is allowing four potential situations to evolve: 1) the defender pulls harder so positional advantage is lost at which point the foul can be called; 2) the offensive player gets to the five meter line and the defender continues to foul leading to a penalty throw; 3) the offensive player takes the ball in and scores; 4) the offensive player takes the ball in but fails to score. Even in this last situation the offensive player was able to take positional advantage and raise it to a probable goal opportunity. In all four outcomes the referee was correct to not call the foul as it raised the attacking advantage of the offense.

Another positional advantage situation could involve a perimeter player being in a good position to receive a pass and a good pass is thrown. If the defender pulls or shoves the perimeter player out of position so that he/she cannot receive the ball, the defender has taken away positional advantage and should be excluded.

Similarly, a defender can have positional advantage. A defender can have his/her hips up and position in the desired driving lane. If an offensive player swims over the defender, the offensive player has violated the defender's positional advantage and should be called for a foul.

Probable Goal Advantage

As the name suggests, a player in position to score a probable goal has probable goal advantage. The player's opportunity to score must be "high percentage" to qualify as probable goal advantage. Here you'll often hear reference to the term "inside water" which refers to the situation where an offensive player's head is closer to the goal than the nearest defender (excluding the goalkeeper). When a defender commits a foul to take away probable goal advantage inside five meters, a penalty foul is called.

Three conditions are usually in place to create probable goal advantage: 1) the player on offense is moving toward the goal; 2) the offensive player has control of the ball; 3) the offensive player has inside water. There may be circumstances where an offensive player is moving toward the goal and has inside water but does not have the ball. If, in this situation, the offensive player is the intended recipient of a good pass then he/she would be deemed to have probable goal advantage.

The position of other defenders can impact probable goal advantage. If a defender recognizes that a teammate has given up goal-side position, that defender can prevent the offensive player from gaining probable goal advantage by getting between the offensive player and the goal, thus taking away inside water and probable goal advantage.

To illustrate probable goal advantage, consider a situation where the set player is at four meters. The set player turns and gets inside water while holding the ball but is tackled by the defense. This is not a foul as the tackle was legal. Now the set drops the ball but remains a major scoring threat because he has inside position and is within reach of the ball. If the defender prevents the set player from picking the ball up and attempting to score, the defender has taken away the set's probable goal advantage and a penalty foul should be called.

Recognizing Good Play

One of the principles of water polo that is least understood by fans is that of recognizing good play. Part of the reason that it is not well recognized is that it does not appear in any rule books. However, considerable attention is given to this topic in the officiating manual. The concept is fairly simple:

"Good play by either team should be rewarded; bad play should be discouraged."

The objective of the team on offense is to score goals. They accomplish this by increasing the level of offensive advantage. Good play includes things like good passing, picks and drives, obtaining positional advantage, demonstrating good ball handling skills and teamwork.

Similarly, the team on defense wants to prevent goals. Good defensive play often includes minimizing the passing lanes the offense can use, staying between the player he/she is guarding and the ball without fouling, and demonstrating that he/she is not fouling. It is also a requirement that the defender show he/she is not committing a foul, particularly at the set position where there is generally a "guilty unless proven innocent" assumption.

The concept of good play is somewhat similar to pass interference in football. In football, a defender that would otherwise be called for pass interference is not penalized if the pass from the quarterback is ruled to be "uncatchable"; for example, it is thrown too far or too high for the receiver to have had a chance of catching it even without the defensive interference.

Let's illustrate good play in water polo using a situation where the ball is passed to the set (offensive player in front of the goal) while two or more defenders are falling back to defend against the set and are about a stroke away. Unless there is a perfect pass and the set has an equal or better chance to get the ball before the defenders, there is no foul. Since there must be other players open when the defenders are falling back, it is not a good offensive play to pass the ball into set and should not, therefore, be rewarded with a foul call against the defense. If, however, it is a perfect pass (good play) leaving the set with a better opportunity to get the ball, a foul should be called if the defense makes illegal contact.

Similarly, you may have a situation where an attacking player with the ball swims into a crowd of defenders. The player chose to swim into a bad situation rather than pass to an open teammate. This is not good play, does not create possessional advantage, and should not be rewarded with a foul even if there is contact from the defenders. The defense should end up with the ball.

Within "good play" there is also a philosophy of "let the offense play." When players try to get position, the ball, and advantage, there is inevitably contact between them. While trying to establish position, some of the contact may constitute a foul. The referee must establish who committed the first foul. Most often this is the defender; in this situation the referee will typically give the attacking player the opportunity to move from a disadvantaged position that was brought on by the defensive foul. In doing so the attacker should not be called for a foul if he is just removing himself from under the defender's foul. In allowing the offensive player maximum opportunity to establish positional advantage, the defense is often given this leeway in being aggressive. Thus, it is not fair to punish the attacking player for something that allows him to play the ball while under this aggressive pressure. Most often this leads to very physical play at the set position in front of the goal.

Sportsmanship

Like most sports, appropriate sportsmanlike behavior is encouraged in water polo. The game of water polo takes it a step further by incorporating sportsmanship into its rules. A player exhibiting inappropriate behavior may be excluded from the remainder of the game with a substitute being allowed only after 20 seconds of time have elapsed from the game clock, or after the other team scores or turns the ball over.

The rules of water polo specifically call out the following as inappropriate behavior:

- use of unacceptable language
- aggressive or persistent foul play
- refusing obedience to or showing disrespect for a referee or official
- behavior against the spirit of the Rules and likely to bring the game into disrepute.

At the collegiate and high school levels referees are specifically given the authority to call an Exclusion Foul against a player for even a minor act of misconduct. The most common example of this foul is making comments to the referee such as: "Call the foul," "He's inside the two," or "Where is the push off?"

If a player commits a minor act of misconduct immediately after being called for an exclusion foul, a penalty throw is awarded.

Overtime and Shootouts

Rules for games that are tied at the end of regulation play vary by tournament, level of play, and governing body. In some cases the game is simply recorded as a tie. In other cases overtime may be used, followed by a penalty shootout if the score remains tied. At other times the game will go into a penalty shootout without using overtime periods.

When overtime is used, it generally consists of a five minute break followed by two periods which are each three minutes in duration. Between the periods there is a two minute break during which the teams change sides.

Generally, under collegiate and high school rules, if the game is tied after the two extra periods a third three minute period is started. However, the format changes to "sudden death" with the first team scoring a goal winning the game (since water polo is now a kinder, gentler sport you may sometimes hear reference to "golden goal" or "sudden victory" rather than "sudden death"). Additional three minute periods will be played until one team scores a goal.

Formerly, during international competition and tournaments using USA Water Polo rules, a penalty shootout took place if two teams were tied after the completion of both overtime periods. In some USA Water Polo sanctioned tournaments the games would go to a shootout, without the use of overtime periods, if a game was tied at the end of regulation time. However, with its 2013 rule modifications, FINA and, thus, USA Water Polo have eliminated the use of overtime periods entirely. Should a game now be tied at the end of regulation time and require a definite result, there will be a penalty shootout to determine the result.

For a shootout each team selects five players and a goalkeeper. The goalkeeper may be substituted during the shootout. Depending on the tournament, the shootout may use both ends of the pool or be conducted at one end of the pool. A coin toss is conducted to determine which team shoots first. Teams then alternate taking penalty throws (see the rules for penalty throws above) until all five players from each team have attempted a shot.

If, after each team has completed its five attempts, the game is still tied, the same five players from each team take alternating shots until one team misses and the other scores.

A Parent's Guide to Water Polo

Official Signals

	The referee lowers the arm from a vertical position to signal: 1) the start of the period (allowing teams to sprint for the ball); 2) to restart after a goal; 3) the go-ahead for the taking of a penalty throw.
	Pointing with one arm, the referee signals the direction of attack for a free throw, goal throw, or corner throw. The other arm points to the spot in the pool where the ball is to be put in play.
	To call a neutral throw the referee points to where the neutral throw will take place then puts both thumbs up (similar to a jump ball in basketball).
	To signal the exclusion of a player, the referee points to the player committing the foul and moves his arm quickly towards the boundary of the field of play. The referee then signals the excluded player's cap number. To exclude two players simultaneously, the referee gives a similar signal, using both hands to signal the simultaneous fouls.
	To exclude a player for misconduct, the referee uses the exclusion signal(s) above. He then rotates his hands round one another (similar to traveling in basketball or illegal procedure in football) to indicate the player is excluded for the game. Generally, that is the only hand signal. However, in the case of brutality, the referee will follow the "roll" signal with crossed arms in front of his body signaling no substitution for four minutes. In both cases the cap number will also be signaled.

Understanding the Game

	When awarding a penalty throw, the referee raises an arm with five fingers in the air (like a student raising her hand in class). The cap number is then signaled to the scorer's table.
	To signal the scoring of a goal, the referee blows a whistle and immediately points to the center of the field of play.
	An exclusion foul for holding is signaled by a motion where the referee holds the wrist of one hand with the other hand.
	An exclusion foul for sinking an opponent is indicated by a downward motion with both hands starting from a horizontal position.
	An exclusion foul for pulling back an opponent is signaled by a pulling motion with both hands vertically extended and pulling towards the referee's body.
	To signal an exclusion foul for kicking the referee makes a kicking movement.
	To signal an exclusion foul for striking an opponent, the referee makes a striking motion with a closed fist starting from a horizontal position.
	When calling an ordinary foul for pushing or pushing off from an opponent, the referee makes a pushing motion away from the body starting from a horizontal position.
	To indicate the ordinary foul of impeding an opponent, the referee makes a crossing motion with one hand horizontally crossing the other. Note: Under FINA rules this is now an exclusion foul.

A Parent's Guide to Water Polo

	When calling the ordinary foul of taking the ball under water (ball under), the referee makes a downward motion with one hand starting from the horizontal position.
	When calling the ordinary foul of standing on the bottom of the pool the referee raises and lowers one foot.
	To signal the ordinary foul of undue delay (taking too long) in taking a free throw, goal throw, or corner throw, the referee raises a hand once or twice with the palm turned upwards.
	When calling a violation of the two meter rule, the referee indicates the number 2 by raising the fore and middle fingers in the air with the arm vertically extended.
	To indicate the ordinary fouls of wasting time or a shot clock violation, the referee moves one hand in a circular motion two or three times and points in the opposite direction.
	To indicate an exclusion foul for a minor act of misconduct (high school, NCAA) the referee rotates one arm in a circular motion.

Signaling Cap Numbers

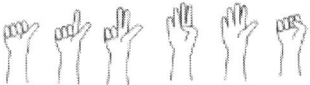

After goals and many types of fouls, referees need to signal who scored the goal or committed the foul. While they may also indicate the number verbally, they should always signal the player's cap number toward the pool and toward the scorer's table. There is a standard approach for signaling the cap number. For numbers one through five, the referee signals the number with one hand and fingers extended to indicate cap number:

1 – Thumb only.
2 – Thumb and forefinger.
3 – Thumb, forefinger, and middle finger.
4 – All fingers except thumb.
5 – All fingers.

To signal numbers from six to nine, the referee shows one hand with five fingers extended and the other hand with additional fingers extended to make up the sum of the players number.

For cap number 10, a clenched fist is shown.

For numbers 11 to 15, a clenched fist is shown with one hand (indicating "10") and the other hand shows additional fingers to make up the cap number (for example, a clenched fist with one hand and the thumb and forefinger extended on the other hand represent cap number 12).

In levels below international competition where higher cap numbers may be used, referees may have to signal caps 16-19. In this case the referee holds up one clenched fist. With the other hand, the referee first holds up five fingers and then raises the other digits as necessary for the cap numbers. So, for example, to show the number 16, the referee will clench the right fist and then show five fingers on the left hand, followed by the thumb on the left hand.

Cap number 20 is indicated by two fists. For cap numbers 21-25, the referee raises two fists and then raises the correct number of fingers on the right hand. If signaling cap numbers 26-29, the referee raises two fists and then raises the correct number of fingers using both hands.

Whistles

The game of water polo moves quickly and you will often miss the referee's hand signal. In many cases, referees don't provide clear hand signals. But, as you become familiar with the game, you'll learn that how the whistle is blown provides an indication as to the type of call being made.

A single whistle, generally very quick, signals an ordinary foul against the defense. Look for the offense to be putting the ball in play immediately with a free throw.

Two whistles usually signal an ordinary foul against the offense. Expect the offensive team to drop the ball and a defensive player to pick it up for a free throw heading the other direction.

Three whistles, usually longer, generally indicate an exclusion or penalty foul. As the third whistle is blown, look for the referee to be pointing toward a player that committed an exclusion foul or holding up five fingers for a penalty shot. Either one of these will be followed by a hand signal indicating the cap number of the player committing the foul.

Water Polo Terminology

Like other sports, and just about every activity in life, water polo comes with its own unique terminology. Over time, after watching enough games, most of the terminology will become second nature to you. However, the faster you become comfortable with words like "five meter line" and "inside water" the easier it will be to understand and appreciate the game and the conversations taking place around you.

While unique to the game of water polo, the terminology in this section is far easier than many of the words in the glossary of your athlete's favorite school text book. And there will be no quiz on these words. But, if you're going to watch water polo, you should learn this vocabulary.

One Two Three Four Five Six	The numbers one through six are often used when referring to positions in the pool. Generally, one and five refer to offensive players in the corners close to the goal line. Six refers to the "set" (player in the middle of the pool and close to the goal). Two, three, and four typically refer to players further from the goal with two and four to the left and right of three.

Attacker	A player whose primary role on the team is offense. Also used, more generically, to refer to any player while on offense (i.e. "the attacker committed an offensive foul").
Back Door	Refers to an offensive player on the "weak side" (the side away from the ball) swimming behind the defender and receiving a pass for a quick shot.
Backhand	A shot taken while the player taking the shot is facing away from the goal. Most often executed by a player in the set position (in front of the goal). This is an exciting shot as it appears to be a blind shot and often comes as a surprise.
Ball Under	An ordinary foul that gives possession to the other team. A Ball Under occurs when a player takes or holds the ball underwater while a defender has body contact with him/her. The player may have been forced by a defender to take the ball underwater or while purposely taking the ball underwater is contacted by a defender; in either case it is a foul against the player with possession of the ball.
Brutality	A serious foul which results in the player being excluded from the remainder of the game. Acts of Brutality include playing in a violent manner, kicking, striking, or attempting to kick or strike with malicious intent. Brutality includes acts against an opponent or official, whether during actual play, during any stoppages, timeouts, after a goal has been scored or during intervals between periods of play.
Cage	Another name for the water polo goal.

Cap	Head wear that all players are required to wear. Caps are used to identify teams (by cap color), individual players (by cap number), and position (goalkeeper caps have different colors than field players).
Cherry Pick	Refers to a player remaining at the offensive end of the pool while his/her team is on defense in hopes of getting an easy goal after a turnover.
Corner Throw	A free entry pass awarded to one team after the opposing team's goalkeeper blocks the ball out of bounds. The pass is initiated from the two meter line, along the side of the pool.
Counter (Attack)	Immediate reaction of offensive team after gaining possession of the ball following a turnover or shot that does not result in a goal. Counter attacks provide an opportunity to get down the pool quickly and attempt a shot before the defense can set-up.
Course	The field of play. Often heard when describing the pool (such as, "they have a 30 meter course").
Dead Time	The time between the referee blowing the whistle to award a free pass and the ball being put back into play. Although action may continue during dead time, the clock does not run. Any foul committed during this time may result in an exclusion.
Delayed Substitution	Refers to situation where one player commits a major foul and is excluded for the remainder of the game. Another player may be put in as a substitute but only after serving the penalty time associated with the foul committed by the first player.

Direct Shot	Generally, after an ordinary foul or an exclusion foul, the team receiving the foul puts the ball in play by throwing a pass. However, if the foul took place outside the five meter line, and the player putting the ball into play picks the ball up and immediately shoots the ball with one motion, it is an allowable "direct shot."
Double Foul	Simultaneous fouls committed by opponents which result in both players being excluded.
Drew Ejection	A statistic that tracks number of times a player causes an opponent to be charged with an exclusion foul. You'll often hear reference to players "drawing" or "earning" an ejection when an opponent commits a foul.
Dribble	A way of moving up the pool while in possession of the ball. While swimming the ball is kept in front of the player's body and in between the arms.
Driver	Front court (offensive) player who, from a position facing his or her opponent, attempts to swim by the opponent to gain a position of advantage.
Dry Pass	A pass that goes from one offensive player to another without the ball touching the water.
Dump the Ball	When the shot clock is near expiration, you'll often hear coaches instruct the team to "dump the ball." This is a direction to throw the ball into an open corner so the team can get back on defense and set-up without a quick counter attack.
Ear Guard	A plastic covering attached to each side of players' caps to provide protection of the ear drum. The ear guard color is required to match the cap color.

Egg Beater	The most common way water polo players stay above water. It is a form of treading water in which the legs move in a circular motion resembling an egg beater. By kicking faster players can get high out of the water for brief periods while attempting to shoot or block the ball.
Ejection	Penalty for committing an exclusion foul. Player must leave the water for 20 seconds or until the other team scores or turns over the ball.
Ejection Area	Space in corner of pool in front of team's bench where player waits while serving an ejection foul.
Exclusion Foul	Refers to a type of foul where the player committing the foul must stay out of the game for 20 seconds or until the other team scores or turns the ball over.
Face Off	Another term for a "neutral throw."
Field Block	A shot that is blocked by a defensive player other than the goalkeeper. Unlike a block by the goalkeeper, a field block that goes past the goal line but not into the goal (goes out bounds) results in a Goal Throw for the defensive team.
Field Player	A player other than the goalkeeper. Any player not wearing a goalkeeper cap is a field player.
Five Meter Line	An imaginary line across the pool five meters in front of the goal. The line is generally marked by a yellow cone, or other type of yellow marker, on the side of the pool. Many water polo rules, such as goalkeeper privileges, taking of penalty throws, taking an immediate shot after a foul, and determining severity of a foul use the five meter line as an important marker.
Five Meter Shot	Another term for "penalty throw."

Fixed Goal	A goal that is attached to the side of the pool. Usually found in older, shorter pools.
Floating Goal	A goal that consists of floats attached to a frame constructed of plastic, fiberglass, and/or aluminum. The goal floats on the surface of the water and is anchored to the side of the pool with lane lines or cords.
Foul	A violation of the rules. Three general types of fouls are ordinary fouls, exclusion fouls, and penalty fouls. The result of a foul is a free throw, an ejection of a player for 20 seconds (or until there is a goal or change of possession), or a penalty throw.
Foul and Drop	A technique where a defender fouls an opponent to stop progress of the ball and then quickly drops back to help defend against another player that may have posed more of a threat.
Foul Out	Refers to a player who has accumulated three personal fouls (exclusion and/or penalty fouls) and is, therefore, excluded for the remainder of the game.
Free Throw (or Free Pass)	Awarded to one team after the other team commits an ordinary foul. The team must make the free throw in a reasonable period (referee's discretion but rule of thumb is three seconds). The throw does not necessarily have to go to another player but the ball must clearly be seen leaving the player's hand.
Front	Refers to a defender getting position in front of the offensive player. Often used to describe when the defender guarding the hole set takes a position between the hole set and his/her team rather than between the hole set and the goal.

Water Polo Terminology

Goal ("The Goal")	A rectangular enclosure measuring 10 feet wide by 3 feet tall. Object of the game is for the offensive team to score by getting the ball into the goal.
Goal (scoring)	When the ball passes completely over the goal line and between the goal posts one point, a "goal", is scored.
Goal Line	An imaginary line at each end of the pool. The line runs parallel to the face of the goal. The ball must pass completely over this line for a goal to be scored. A ball passing completely over this line but outside the goal posts results in a goal throw for the defending team.
Goal Throw	A free throw taken by any defensive player from inside the two meter line after the ball crosses the goal line without going into the goal (unless last touched by the goalkeeper). Goal throws are almost always taken by the goalkeeper.
Goalie Cap	A unique cap that identifies the goalie. Typically the cap is red or has quarter panels of red and a team color. Depending on level of play, goalie caps either start with the number 1 (1, 1A, 1B, etc) or display number 13.
Goalie or Goalkeeper	Player responsible for defending the goal. Rules provide goalies with special privileges when they are inside the five meter line. Privileges include use of both hands when attempting to block the ball and standing on the bottom of the pool (if the pool is shallow).
Goalie Out	An alert sometimes heard during games. It alerts offensive players that the opposing goalie has ventured out of the immediate goal area and is not in a strong position to block a shot.

Half Distance Line	An imaginary line at the middle of the course that divides the playing area into equal halves. At the start of each quarter players sprint for the ball which is either placed at, or dropped by the referee on, the half distance line.
Half Tank	In the area of the half distance line.
Help Inside	An alert to defensive players to help teammates that are getting beat by an offensive player inside five meters or near the goal.
Help the Ball	A called reminder to offensive players to help a teammate that is under pressure with the ball and having trouble finding a teammate to receive a pass.
High Corner	Top left and right corners of the goal. This is frequently the target when an offensive player is taking a shot from outside.
Hips Up	Coaches are often heard encouraging players to get their "hips up." This refers to getting good position against the opponent by getting hips high with the body in an almost prone position.
Hole Set	An offensive position where the player is typically positioned near the two meter line in front of the opponent's goal. This is generally a very physical position having a great deal of contact with the defender. Often referred to as the "hole" or the "set".
Inside Water	Offensive player having position where there is no defender between him/her and the goalie. Having inside water is important in determining positional advantage when referees are making foul calls.
Interference	Disrupting or interfering with an opponent's free throw. Results in an ejection for the player committing the interference foul.

Kick-Out	Another term for "ejection."
Major Foul	An "exclusion foul."
Man Down	Alert call to defensive team when one player has been ejected to let other defensive players know that they have one less player in the water. You'll often hear coach or goalie yell "we're down."
Man Up	Alert call to offensive players when a player from the other team has been ejected to let other offensive players know they have a player advantage in the water. You'll often hear coach or goalie yell "we're up."
Mid-Tank	In the area of the half distance line.
Nail Check	Pre-game check performed by referee to ensure that finger and toe nails of players don't constitute a hazard.
Neutral Throw	Used by referee when it is not clear which team should have possession of the ball. Referee drops the ball in a position where one player from each team has an equal opportunity to gain possession of the ball. Other players must remain two meters away from the players involved in the neutral throw until at least one of them has touched the ball.
Offensive Advantage	An offensive player has offensive advantage when he/she has established position between the defender and the defender's goal (see "inside water").
Offensive Foul	A foul committed by the offensive team. Results in the ball being turned over to the opposing team.

Ordinary Foul	A foul such as holding, obstructing, or sinking committed against a player not in contact with the ball and not holding offensive advantage. Most fouls in water polo are ordinary fouls which result in a free throw for the other team. Play continues after the foul call and the team awarded the free throw must put the ball in play quickly (generally within three seconds).
Passing Lanes	Imaginary line between player with ball and other offensive players where the ball would be passed. Defense will often focus on cutting off the passing lanes.
Penalty Area	Area at end of pool in front of team's bench where players are to remain after an ejection until the penalty time is over.
Penalty Foul	A foul for which the opponent is awarded a Penalty Throw. Most common Penalty Foul is a defensive foul against a player inside the five meter line in a situation where "a goal probably would have resulted." Other fouls such as displacing the goal, attempting to block a shot with two hands, or the goalkeeper taking the ball under water also qualify as Penalty Fouls.
Penalty Throw (Shot)	A free shot against only the goalie awarded to one team after the opponent has been called for a Penalty Foul. Shot is taken from the five meter line on the referee's signal (blowing of whistle and dropping of raised arm). Shot must be taken in one uninterrupted movement.
Personal Foul	Exclusion fouls and penalty fouls are tracked as personal fouls against the individual player that committed the foul. Once a player accumulates three personal fouls he/she is excluded from the remainder of the game. Ordinary fouls do not count as personal fouls.

Water Polo Terminology

Post (Goal)	The vertical bars on each side of the goal. Shots that hit the "post" are really close but went just a little wide.
Post (position)	A position on the two meter line in front of the goal post.
Press Defense	Defensive approach where the defensive players play very tight on offensive players to make passing or driving more difficult.
Pumping the Ball	Technique where an offensive player moves his/her arm to simulate a shot in an attempt to get the goalkeeper to commit to a block before the offensive player takes a different shot.
Red Card	Card is shown by referee when a bench player or coach exhibits inappropriate behavior. Anyone receiving a red card must leave the bench area and may not communicate with the team.
Re-Entry Area	Area at end of field of play where players exit and enter the game. A player entering or exiting the field of play through another spot while the game is in progress may be charged with a foul.
Release	After the ball has been turned over you often hear the goalie yelling for a teammate to "release." This is a request for someone to make a cut and look back for a pass from the goalkeeper.
Save	A block of an offensive player's shot by the opposing goalkeeper.
Set	Often used when referring to the "Hole Set".

Shoot Out	A method of determining a winner when a game is still tied after regulation time and any overtime periods are completed. Each team selects five shooters; teams alternate attempting penalty throws with the team that scores more goals during the shootout winning the game. If, after each of the five players from each team have attempted their shots, the game is still tied the shootout continues with one shooter from each team until one team scores a goal and the other team fails to score on its attempt.
Shot Clock	Clock found at each end of the pool deck that shows time remaining for offensive team to take a shot. If the shot clock expires before a shot is attempted, or a foul called, the ball is turned over to the other team. Shot clock is generally 30 seconds.
Slough	A defensive perimeter player dropping back, sometimes after intentionally committing an ordinary foul, to help guard the Hole Set.
Sprint	At the start of each period, each team lines up on its own goal line. At the referees signal they sprint toward the middle of the pool where the referee drops the ball (in some pools, particularly in international competition, the ball is already positioned in the middle of the pool). The team who has a player get to the ball first can control it and get the first offensive possession of the period.
Strong Side	The side of the pool (left or right of the goalie) where the ball is located.
Tackle	Defensive touching or grabbing of an offensive player who has the ball in his/her hand. This is a legal maneuver.

Water Polo Terminology

Two Meter Line	Imaginary straight line across the pool that runs two meters in front of the goal line. Offensive players are not allowed to cross this line (an ordinary foul) unless the ball is past the line.
Walk It In	Coaches and teammates will frequently urge an offensive player to "walk it in." This is telling the player with the ball to keep moving toward the goal. Generally this happens when there is no defender near the player with the ball, giving the offensive player an opportunity to create a scoring opportunity by just getting closer to the goal.
Wall Goal	Another term for "fixed goal."
Weak (Side)	The weak side is the side of the pool (left or right of the goalkeeper) where the ball is not located. You'll often hear coaches and other offensive players calling "weak" to let the person with the ball know that there is a teammate with a potentially open shot at the goal on the opposite side of the pool.
Wet Pass	A pass that goes from one offensive player which lands in the water as it is received. It is very common for the goalkeeper to intentionally throw a wet pass on a counter attack. This is also the type of pass frequently used to get the ball to the hole set.
Wing Out	Another term for "release". Wing Out refers to a player swimming up the field of play turning out toward the side of the field of play to create a passing opportunity, usually coming from the goalie.
Yellow Card	Shown by a referee to a coach or player to indicate he/she has officially been warned for misconduct. A second yellow card in a game has the same effect as a red card.

Water Polo After High School

So, your son or daughter has fallen for water polo and can't imagine not playing the game after high school. If he or she is a star there may be opportunities at an NCAA Division I program. But, even if that option is not in the cards, there are other options for athletes that have a strong interest in playing beyond high school.

A number of colleges and universities offer intercollegiate water polo programs (see Table 1). At the Division 1 (DI) and Division 2 (DII) levels, schools are allowed to give athletic scholarships. However, less than 2% of high school athletes go on to receive athletic scholarships to college. Contributing to the small number of available athletic scholarships are limits the NCAA places on the number of scholarships schools are allowed to award in each sport. In men's water polo schools are limited to $4^1/_2$ scholarships while in women's water polo they are limited to 8 scholarships. These are maximum numbers; not all schools in those two divisions give out the maximum number of awards. When scholarships are awarded they are often partial scholarships. Thus, a school could have 16 athletes sharing 8 scholarships.

Water polo players that are not recruited to play water polo may choose to "walk-on" and attempt to secure a spot on the team. Schools may even help an athlete interested in walking on through the application process without making any financial support commitment.

Division 3 (DIII) schools are another option for students looking for an opportunity to continue their water polo careers. These schools are not permitted to provide athletic scholarships but provide another avenue for students looking for a place to continue playing water polo.

In addition to traditional intercollegiate competition, many schools have club water polo teams that compete against other schools' club teams (see Table 2 and Table 3). The club team may be in addition to the intercollegiate team or may be the only water polo option at a particular school. Club teams don't provide financial assistance but do provide another option for athletes hoping to find a place to continue playing competitive water polo.

Yet another option for collegiate water polo exists at the community college level (Table 4). For students in California, or wanting to move to California, there are many schools in the community college system offering competitive water polo programs.

As with all sports, the opportunities to continue competing in water polo do diminish as players get older. However, if there is a strong desire to continue playing there are options. As outlined above, there are several levels of intercollegiate competition, clubs, and community college avenues an athlete can pursue. But even if youth and high school water polo mark the end of an athlete's water polo journey, he or she will have gained the physical benefits of training, had the opportunity to be challenged competitively, learned to be part of a team, and developed time management and self-discipline skills that can last a lifetime.

Table 1 - Intercollegiate Programs

School	Men's Div	Men's Affiliation	Women's Div	Women's Affiliation
Arizona State University Tempe, AZ	----	----	DI	Mountain Pacific Sports Federation
Azusa Pacific University Azusa, CA	----	----	DII	Golden Coast Conference
Brown University Providence, RI	DI	Collegiate Water Polo Association	DI	Collegiate Water Polo Association
Bucknell University Lewisburg, PA	DI	Collegiate Water Polo Association	DI	Collegiate Water Polo Association
California Baptist University Riverside, CA	DII	Western Water Polo Association	DII	Golden Coast Conference
California Institute of Technology Pasadena, CA	DIII	Southern California Intercollegiate Athletic Conf	DIII	Southern California Intercollegiate Athletic Conf
California Lutheran University Thousand Oaks, CA	DIII	Southern California Intercollegiate Athletic Conf	DIII	Southern California Intercollegiate Athletic Conf
California State University, Monterey Bay Seaside, CA	----	----	DII	Western Water Polo Association Women

School	Men's Div	Men's Affiliation	Women's Div	Women's Affiliation
California State University, Bakersfield Bakersfield, CA	---	---	DI	Western Water Polo Association
California State University, East Bay Hayward, CA	---	---	DII	Western Water Polo Association
California State University, Northridge Northridge, CA	---	---	DI	Big West Conference
California State University, San Bernardino San Bernardino, CA	---	---	DII	Western Water Polo Association
Carthage College Kenosha, WI	---	---	DIII	Collegiate Water Polo Association
Chapman University Orange, CA	DIII	Southern California Intercollegiate Athletic Conference	DIII	Southern California Intercollegiate Athletic Conference
Claremont McKenna – Harvey Mudd – Scripps Colleges Claremont, CA	DIII	Southern California Intercollegiate Athletic Conference	DIII	Southern California Intercollegiate Athletic Conference
Colorado State University Fort Collins, CO	---	---	DI	Western Water Polo Association
Concordia University Irvine Irvine, CA	NAIA	---	NAIA	---

Table 1 – Intercollegiate Programs

School	Men's Div	Men's Affiliation	Women's Div	Women's Affiliation
Connecticut College New London, CT	DIII	Collegiate Water Polo Association	DIII	Collegiate Water Polo Association
Fordham University Bronx, NY	DI	Collegiate Water Polo Association	---	---
Fresno Pacific University Fresno, CA	DII	Western Water Polo Association	DII	Golden Coast Conference
Gannon University Erie, PA	DII	Collegiate Water Polo Association	DII	Collegiate Water Polo Association
George Washington University Washington DC	DI	Collegiate Water Polo Association	DI	Collegiate Water Polo Association
Grove City College Grove City, PA	---	---	DIII	Collegiate Water Polo Association
Hartwick College Oneonta, NY	---	---	DI	Collegiate Water Polo Association
Harvard University Boston, MA	DI	Collegiate Water Polo Association	DI	Collegiate Water Polo Association
Indiana University Bloomington, IN	---	---	DI	Collegiate Water Polo Association
Iona College New Rochelle, NY	DI	Collegiate Water Polo Association	DI	Metro Atlantic Athletic Conference
Johns Hopkins University Baltimore, MD	DIII	Collegiate Water Polo Association	---	---
Long Beach State University Long Beach, CA	DI	Mountain Pacific Sports Federation	DI	Big West Conference

School	Men's Div	Men's Affiliation	Women's Div	Women's Affiliation
Loyola Marymount University, Los Angeles, CA	DI	Western Water Polo Association	DI	Golden Coast Conference
Macalester College, St Paul, MN	---	---	DIII	Collegiate Water Polo Association
Marist College, Poughkeepsie, NY	---	---	DI	Metro Atlantic Athletic Conference
Massachusetts Institute of Technology, Cambridge, MA	DIII	Collegiate Water Polo Association	---	---
Mercyhurst University, Erie, PA	DII	Collegiate Water Polo Association	DII	Collegiate Water Polo Association
Monmouth College, Monmouth, IL	DIII	Collegiate Water Polo Association	DIII	Collegiate Water Polo Association
Notre Dame College (Ohio), Cleveland, OH	DII	Collegiate Water Polo Association	DII	Collegiate Water Polo Association
Occidental College, Los Angeles, CA	DIII	Southern California Intercollegiate Athletic Conference	DIII	Southern California Intercollegiate Athletic Conference
Pennsylvania State University, Erie, the Behrend College, Erie, PA	DIII	Alleghany Mountain Collegiate Conference	DIII	Collegiate Water Polo Association
Pepperdine University, Malibu, CA	DI	Mountain Pacific Sports Federation	---	---

Table 1 – Intercollegiate Programs

School	Men's Div	Men's Affiliation	Women's Div	Women's Affiliation
Pomona-Pitzer Colleges Claremont, CA	DIII	Southern California Intercollegiate Athletic Conf	DIII	Southern California Intercollegiate Athletic Conf
Princeton University Princeton, NJ	DI	Collegiate Water Polo Association	DI	Collegiate Water Polo Association
Salem International University Salem, WV	DII	Collegiate Water Polo Association	DII	Collegiate Water Polo Association
San Diego State University San Diego, CA	----	----	DI	Golden Coast Conference
San Jose State University San Jose, CA	----	----	DI	Mountain Pacific Sports Federation
Santa Clara University Santa Clara, CA	DI	Western Water Polo Association	DI	Golden Coast Conference
Siena College Loudonville, NY	----	----	DI	Metro Atlantic Athletic Conference
Sonoma State University Rohnert Park, CA	----	----	DII	Western Water Polo Association
St. Francis College (New York) Brooklyn Heights, NY	DI	Collegiate Water Polo Association	DI	Metro Atlantic Athletic Conference
Stanford University Stanford, CA	DI	Mountain Pacific Sports Federation	DI	Mountain Pacific Sports Federation
US Air Force Academy Colorado Springs, CO	DI	Western Water Polo Association	----	----
US Naval Academy Annapolis, MD	DI	Collegiate Water Polo Association	----	----

School	Men's Div	Men's Affiliation	Women's Div	Women's Affiliation
University of California, Berkeley Berkeley, CA	DI	Mountain Pacific Sports Federation	DI	Mountain Pacific Sports Federation
University of California, Davis Davis, CA	DI	Western Water Polo Association	DI	Big West Conference
University of California, Irvine Irvine, CA	DI	Mountain Pacific Sports Federation	DI	Big West Conference
University of California, Los Angeles Los Angeles, CA	DI	Mountain Pacific Sports Federation	DI	Mountain Pacific Sports Federation
University of California, San Diego La Jolla, CA	DII	Western Water Polo Association	DII	Western Water Polo Association
University of California, Santa Barbara Santa Barbara, CA	DI	Mountain Pacific Sports Federation	DI	Big West Conference
University of Hawaii, Manoa Honolulu, HI	----	----	DI	Big West Conference
University of La Verne La Verne, CA	DIII	Southern California Intercollegiate Athletic Conf	DIII	Southern California Intercollegiate Athletic Conf
University of Michigan Ann Arbor, MI	----	----	DI	Collegiate Water Polo Association
University of Redlands Redlands, CA	DIII	Southern California Intercollegiate Athletic Conf	DIII	Southern California Intercollegiate Athletic Conf

Table 1 – Intercollegiate Programs

School	Men's Div	Men's Affiliation	Women's Div	Women's Affiliation
University of Southern California Los Angeles, CA	DI	Mountain Pacific Sports Federation	DI	Mountain Pacific Sports Federation
University of the Pacific Stockton, CA	DI	Mountain Pacific Sports Federation	DI	Golden Coast Conference
Utica College Utica, NY	----	----	DIII	Collegiate Water Polo Association
Villanova University Villanova, PA	----	----	DI	Metro Atlantic Athletic Conference
Virginia Military Institute Lexington, VA	----	----	DI	Metro Atlantic Athletic Conference
Wagner College Staten Island, NY	----	----	DI	Metro Atlantic Athletic Conference
Washington & Jefferson College Washington, PA	DIII	Collegiate Water Polo Association	DIII	Collegiate Water Polo Association
Whittier College Whittier, CA	DIII	Southern California Intercollegiate Athletic Conf	DIII	Southern California Intercollegiate Athletic Conf

Table 2 - CWPA Men's Clubs

Amherst College
Arizona State University
Auburn University
Augustana College
Bates College
Baylor University
Baylor University
Binghamton University
Bloomsburg University
Boston College
Boston University
Bowdoin College
Bucknell University
California Polytechnic State University
California State University-Chico
California State University-Maritime Academy
Carleton College
Carnegie Mellon University
Central Washington University
Clemson University
Colby College
Colgate University
Columbia University
Cornell University
Dartmouth College
Drexel University
Duke University
Emory University
Florida Gulf Coast University
Florida Institute of Technology
Florida International University
Florida State University
Franklin & Marshall College
Georgetown University
Georgia Tech University
Grand Valley State University
Grinnell College
Grove City College
Hamilton College
Illinois State University
Indiana University
Iowa State University
James Madison University
Kansas State University
Knox College
La Salle University
Lehigh University
Lindenwood University
Louisianna State University
Loyola University
Loyola University
Macalester College
Marquette University
Miami University
Michigan State University
Middlebury College
Millersville University
Monmouth College
New York University
North Carolina State University
Northwestern University
Ohio University
Oregon State University
Pennsylvania State University
Portland State University
Purdue University
Rensselaer Polytechnic Institute
Rice University
Saint Joseph's University
Saint Mary's College
Saint Michaels College
San Diego State University
San Jose State University
Seattle University
Southern Illinois University
St. John's University (Minn.)
St. Louis University
St. Mary's University (Minn.)
Stanford University
Syracuse University
Texas A&M University
Texas State University
Texas Tech University
The Ohio State University
Trinity University
Tuffs University
US Coast Guard Academy
United States Military Academy

United States Naval Academy
University of Arizona
University of California- Santa Barbara
University of California-Berkeley
University of California-Davis
University of California-Irvine
University of California-Los Angeles
University of California-San Diego
University of California-Santa Cruz
University of Central Florida
University of Chicago
University of Colorado
University of Dayton
University of Delaware
University of Denver
University of Florida
University of Georgia
University of Houston
University of Illinois
University of Illinois-Chicago
University of Iowa
University of Maryland
University of Massachusetts
University of Miami
University of Michigan
University of Minnesota
University of Nebraska
University of New Mexico
University of North Carolina
University of Notre Dame
University of Oregon
University of Pennsylvania
University of Pittsburgh
University of San Diego
University of Southern California
University of Tennessee
University of Texas, Austin
University of Utah
University of Vermont
University of Virginia
University of Washington
University of Wisconsin
University of Wyoming
Vanderbilt University
Villanova University
Virginia Polytechnic Institute & State University
Washington University in St. Louis
Wesleyan University
Western Illinois University
Williams College
Yale University

Table 3 - CWPA Women's Clubs

Arizona State University
Bates College
Baylor University
Boston College
Boston University
Bowdoin College
California Polytechnic State University
California State University, Chico
California State University, Maritime Academy
Carleton College
Colgate University
Colorado College
Colorado State University
Columbia University
Cornell University
Dartmouth College
Duke University
Emory University
Florida International University
Florida State University
Grand Valley State University
Grinnell College
Illinois State University
Indiana University
Iowa State University
James Madison University
Knox College
Lindenwood University
Loyola Marymount University
Massachusetts Institute of Technology
Miami University (Ohio)
Michigan State University
Middlebury College
New York University
Northern Arizona University
Ohio University
Oregon State University
Pennsylvania State University
Pepperdine University
Purdue University
Rice University
Saint Mary's College (Calif.)
San Diego State University
Syracuse University
Texas A&M University
Texas State University
Texas Tech University
Trinity University
U. S. Air Force Academy
University of Arizona
University of California, Berkeley
University of California, Davis
University of California, Irvine
University of California, Los Angeles
University of California, San Diego
University of Central Florida
University of Colorado
University of Florida
University of Georgia
University of Illinois
University of Iowa
University of Miami
University of Michigan
University of New Mexico
University of North Carolina
University of Notre Dame
University of Oregon
University of Pennsylvania
University of Pittsburgh
University of Richmond
University of Southern California
University of Texas, Austin
University of Utah
University of Virginia
University of Washington
University of Wisconsin
Virginia Tech
Washington University (Mo.)
Wellesley College
West Chester University
Western Oregon University
Western Washington University
Williams College
Yale University

Table 4 - Community College Water Polo

School	Men's	Women's
American River College Sacramento, CA	Big 8	Big 8
Cabrillo College Aptos, CA	Coast Conference	Coast Conference
Cerritos College Norwalk, CA	South Coast Conference	South Coast Conference
Chaffey College Rancho Cucamonga, CA	South Coast Conference	South Coast Conference
Citrus College Glendora, CA	Western State Conference	Western State Conference
College of San Mateo San Mateo, CA	-----	Coast Conference
Cuesta College San Luis Obispo, CA	Western State Conference	Western State Conference
Cypress College Cypress, CA	-----	Orange Empire
De Anza College Cupertino, CA	Coast Conference	Coast Conference
Diablo Valley College Pleasant Hill, CA	Big 8	Big 8
El Camino Community College Torrance, CA	South Coast Conference	South Coast Conference
Foothill College Los Altos Hills, CA	-----	Coast Conference
Fresno City College Fresno, CA	-----	Big 8
Fullerton College Fullerton, CA	Orange Empire	Orange Empire
Golden West College Huntington Beach, CA	Orange Empire	Orange Empire
Grossmont College El Cajon, CA	Pacific Coast	Pacific Coast
Laney College Oakland, CA	-----	Coast Conference
Long Beach City College Long Beach, CA	South Coast Conference	South Coast Conference
Los Angeles Pierce College Woodland Hills, CA	-----	Western State Conference

School	Men's	Women's
Los Angeles Trade Technical College Los Angeles, CA	South Coast Conference	South Coast Conference
Los Angeles Valley College Valley Glen, CA	Western State Conference	Western State Conference
Merced College Merced, CA	Coast Conference	Coast Conference
Modesto Junior College Modesto, CA	Big 8	Big 8
Mt. San Antonio College Walnut, CA	South Coast Conference	South Coast Conference
Ohlone College Fremont, CA	Coast Conference	Coast Conference
Orange Coast College Costa Mesa, CA	Orange Empire	Orange Empire
Palomar College San Marco, CA	Pacific Coast	Pacific Coast
Pasadena City College Pasadena, CA	-----	South Coast Conference
Rio Hondo College Whittier, CA	-----	South Coast Conference
Riverside Community College Riverside, CA	Orange Empire	Orange Empire
Sacramento City College Sacramento, CA	-----	Big 8
Saddleback College Mission Viejo, CA	Orange Empire	Orange Empire
San Diego Mesa College San Diego, CA	Pacific Coast	Pacific Coast
San Diego Miramar College San Diego, CA	-----	Pacific Coast
San Joaquin Delta College Stockton, CA	Big 8	Big 8
Santa Ana College Santa Ana, CA	Orange Empire	Orange Empire
Santa Monica College Santa Monica, CA	Western State Conference	Western State Conference

Table 4 – Community College Water Polo

School	Men's	Women's
Santa Rosa Junior College Santa Rosa, CA	Big 8	Big 8
Sierra College Rocklin, CA	Big 8	Big 8
Southwestern College Chula Vista, CA	Pacific Coast	Pacific Coast
Ventura College Ventura, CA	Western State Conference	Western State Conference
West Valley College Saratoga, CA	Coast Conference	Coast Conference

Made in the USA
San Bernardino, CA
23 June 2015